Songs of Life

Songs of Life

(Collection of Poems)

Dr. A.P.J. Abdul Kalam

Published by
PRABHAT PRAKASHAN PVT. LTD.
4/19 Asaf Ali Road,
New Delhi-110 002 (INDIA)
e-mail: prabhatbooks@gmail.com

ISBN 978-93-90366-26-2
SONGS OF LIFE
poems by Dr. A.P.J. Abdul Kalam

Edition
2026

Price
₹ 250.00 (Rupees Two Hundred Fifty only)

Printed at
R-Tech Offset Printers, Delhi

Author's Note

The ***Songs of Life*** is presented with selected poems from my books of poem **Life Tree**, **Luminous Sparks** and **My Journey**, and also some of my new poems. The purpose of this Songs of Life is to celebrate the human life. Inspite of many sufferings all around, God has blessed us with his grace in multiple dimensions of nature smiling at us. Hence, Songs of Life is the Song of every heart and soul in happiness and in sorrow. The result of the poems should be to cheer our hearts.

Contents

Contents

Are We Alone

Oh, my human race,
How, we were born,
In the Universe of near infinity,
Are we alone?

I was seeking answer for the great
Question of creation, weighing heavy
My mind as I am in seventieth orbit
Around sun, my little habitat, the star
Where my race living, lived billions of years

And will live billions of years, till the
  sun shines.

This is the millennium question of
  humanity,

And sought the help of our creator, to
  know

Are we alone?

On the eventful day, I was flying

The earth below me, the human
  habitat

Vanished in the white river of cloud,

Silent, turbulent free everywhere the divine
Splendour reflecting.
On the above, the full moon with its magnificent might,
My heart melted, my friend co-passenger
Vidyasagar[1] joined in the heavenly display.
The beauty entered into our soul
And blossomed happiness into our mind and body.
We the humanity bowed to the heavenly answer,
We are not alone, billion of billion of lives
Of various forms spring in the planets of
Galaxy after galaxies.
Then the dawn of divine message.

1. My scientist friend

There was the divine echo in the full moon night
From my creator.
Shaken, bewildered and wondered
The echo engulfed me and my race
"You, the human race is the best of my creation
You will live and live.
You give and give till you are united,
In human happiness and pain.
My bliss will be born in you
Love is continuum.
That is the mission of humanity,
You will see every day in Life Tree
You learn and learn
My best of creations."
Beautiful morning it was,
Sun radiating, driving away the clouds

Parrots and Kokilas were at their
musical flight
We the yellow heaven group[2] entered
Flower garden of Asiad
Roses were in their splendour
Radiating beauty in White and
Crimson
Bowing to the dawn of sun

2. My walking friends at Asiad Village

We walked and walked, our feet on the green
Meadow giving velvet touch,
Children somewhere ringing in unison in their innocence
Peacocks in the background giving beautiful display.

There was a majestic scene of Life Tree
Cluster of tall and straight Nag phalli grove[3]

3. Plant with multiple layers, blossoms one layer after another layer

Undaunted to the sun rays direction

Multi layered, each flower plant bubbling with life,

We approached very close to the happy plants

Astonished to see the nature's wonder.

Bottom layers have shed the flower all around the sand

Whereas mid layer flower blossomed

In number to the magnificence

Perfume radiating, beauty all around

Honey bees filling the flower bed, mutual love flowing

Intoxicated with the scene, we looked at the top layer

Ring of the buds about to blossom

And new layers at their birth.

Again the great divine echo enters all around us
"Flowers blossom, radiate beauty and spread perfume
And give honey. On the eve of life
Flowers silently fall to the earth, they belong.
Oh my creation this is mission of human life
You are born, live life of giving
And bond the human life
Your mission is the Life Tree.
My blessings to you my creation
In my own planet of billion Galaxies."

Oh my human race
Let's sing the song of creation.

[Composed at ASIAD Village Complex on 14 January 2001]

□

The Great Tree In My Home

Oh my home tree[4],

You are great, among trees,

How many, many generations were enriched

Through decades of your help, so kind,

Many now live under your sagely care,

Your song of life, I love to hear.

4. Indian name of the tree—Arjuna, Botanical name—Terminalia

Oh my friend Kalam,

I crossed age hundred like your father and mother.

Everyday morning, you walk an hour

I also see you on full moon nights,

Walking with a thinking mood.

I know my friend, the thoughts in your mind,

"What can I give".

When in April, you look at me,

Again and again with deep concern,

Seeing me shedding leaves in thousands and thousands,

You ask me my friend,

What is my burden?

Leaves I shed to give birth to new leaves,

Flowers bloom attracting butterflies and bees.

So, Kalam, it is not burden for me,

It is a beautiful phase of my life.

Now Kalam, take a tour with me,

See closely inside, in my dense branches,

A large beehive full of honey,

Built by thousands of worker bees,

Honey collected by their ceaseless work.

Honey-hive so heavy, with sweet honey drops,

Guarded well by thousands of bees.
For whom, this honey is collected and guarded,
It is for you many rich and poor,
Our mission is to give to every life.

Oh Kalam, did you see so many nests,
Built by various birds in various parts of my branches.
Most of the top branches of my tree attract,
Hundreds of parrots as their home.
You have rightly called me parrots' tree.

Nowadays, you call me also honey tree,
When I hear talking to your grandson about me,
I smile and smile.
I give many homes to birds in my branches and trunk holes.
I have heard songs of birds, and seen, love, birth and growth.
The birds are flying and flying around me sharing happiness.
And also, sometimes, with fear for eagles!

Nowadays, Kalam, daily during your walk,
You come close to me to see my root,
All-around dense flower garden with a velvet grass bed.
To a peahen,

The peahen giving warmth to the eggs.

All the time giving safe breeding with motherly love.

It was beautiful sight in your home.

The peahen with its seven kids,

Majestically walking now all around me,

And guarding the children day and night.

Now, you question Kalam, what is my mission?

Mission of hundred years of my life.

My mission, I enjoy giving what all I have,

I share, flower and honey, give abode,
for hundred of birds, and to human beings.

I give and give.

So, I remain, young and happy, always.

[Poem presented at a Poets' Meet at Queen's University Belfast, Northern Ireland on 10th June 2009]

□

What Can I give

1. **One evening, a beautiful evening**

   I was in a mission of thanks giving

   to my families of nature.

   Reached the hut in the mughal garden

   In the midst of dense banyan grove.

   Herbal fragrance filled all around,

   Musical fountain with rhythm of Shehnai.

   Hundreds of intoxicated parrots by the music.

One young banyan tree, talked to me "O! Kalam

See us in all seasons, with trunks rooted on earth

We absorb all the heat in the mid days

We give shelter to so many birds.

Give shadow and cool breeze

to animals and humans all around.

What man gives, tell me Kalam."

"O my young friend, you have given

A great message of Giving,

Continue your God's mission of giving and giving."

2. **Suddenly many parrots came and sat**

All around the branches of the trees

In the serene banyan grove,

Lighted the place beautiful and glittering.

One parrot, shot a question to me,

"We the parrots are beautiful!

As your poetic words picture us

O Kalam, can you fly on your own?"

"O! No my friends, you are blessed,

Continue the mission of spreading happiness"

My human pride completely melted.

3. A new scene emerged

With a family of eight peacocks and peahens,

Surrounding me seated in the hut

Three of the peacocks with fully unfurled wings

Danced and danced, it was a heavenly sight,

Never seen, three peacocks in my garden,

All dancing in a place same time,

Time stood still.

A younger one looked at me

"Kalam sir, can you remember me?"

"O friend, you are all alike."

Peacock said, I was the one lying semiconscious

In front of your office, you brought the doctor, Sudhir

You touched me with kindness.

Then I did not know anything,

Except I was on the operation table of Sudhir.

The tumor in my throat was removed,

Medicine given and I was fed and cured.

The doctor handed over me to you,

You blessed me and let me fly.

In bio-diversity park with happiness rising

Today Kalam sir, we gave you

A final thanks giving dance."

"O my young friend,

God has blessed you with

A great quality called gratitude

Continue spreading it wherever you go!"

4. **Entered into the bio-diversity park**

Deer herds with their little ones

They ran and ran,

the leader marching with horns straight,

Glanced at me and, said "I am the leader of the deers"

Then there was a formation of deers,

The horned leader was bowing his head

Then a miracle happened.

One lovely deer, a young one slowly and

slowly advanced towards me,

And started licking my hand

Looked at me, said " I am the little one

You fed me daily with milk,
When my mother forsaken me,

As I could not walk and run reach my mother's

Thank you sir, feeding me milk many a days and for curing my injuries.

You and Sudhir made a deer out of me"

This event electrified me, the deer herd slowly advanced

Bowed with tears rolling,

From the return of kindness.

5. **Sun was setting,**

Full moon was rising from the horizon

Spiritual garden was welcoming,

O' Kalam we have a message for you

We are family of dates, olive, tulsi trees.

And many more,

You see us we grow together

We live together,
Muslims, Christians, and Hindus,
and those from other religions
Adore us, individually.
Breeze embraces us,
In all seasons,
We give freshness and fragrance.
Kalam, you can tell about us,
To all your human citizens"
O! My spiritual gurus
You are indeed giving

A great message on Unity of minds

That was indeed for me

Treat, from university of learning

I got answer, what can I give.

6. **The nature's citizens inspired,**

What can I give?

Yes, removing the sorrow of the needy,

Gladdening of the sad heart,

And above all, I realized in giving,

Happiness radiates all around.

[Composed at the Mughal Garden On the eve of farewell to Presidential post on 24 July 2007]

□

Noble Nation[5]

A beautiful and yet distinct
Reddish light engulfed the galaxy,
The Milky Way, our galaxy.
All the stars surprised with the alarm,
Where from this lovely powerful light,
Who emanates, who emanates
That was the cry of the galaxy.

5. Poem from the book ***'Family And The Nation'*** authored by Dr. Kalam & Acharya Mahapragya

I will answer, my friends

"Oh my galaxy friends, I am the sun,

I have eight planets in orbit,

One of them is earth,

Carries six billion human lives.

They live in hundreds of nations.

One of the nations with great civilization,

India 2020, celebrates the birth of the noble nation.

Light of celebration from India reaching our galaxy

Nation with clean environment without pollution,

Having prosperity without poverty,

Peace without fear of war,

A happiest place to live".

□

Oceans Meet

"I am the Island of Rameswaram, dear friend,

Born out of the shining water of the Indian Ocean.

O my fellow Island, O my dearest friend,

What is your origin and where do you live?"

"Dear Ramy, they call me Formosa[6] – the beautiful Island,

I live like a beautiful flower seeing the early sun-rise,

6. Formosa in Taiwan

Sitting in the gardens of magnificent oceans of the pacific,

As the deepest waves of the noble ocean embrace me with affection."

"O friend, my dear friend – Formosa,

I greet you with a heart brimming with joy.

My vast ocean embraces a land of ancient religions, culture and divine wisdom,

It is the soil where enlightened one–

Lord Buddha once walked upon."

"O Ramy! You are indeed showered with blessings divine,
Garlanding around me are nations with billions of human souls,
It was, the land and the nation which I call mine,
That gave birth to the wisest sage, Confucius shaped human thoughts for noble ways of life."

And then the two great humble oceans prayed and prayed,
The two noble sages, then descended like angels upon the Sangam[7],
The magnificent oceans then prayed to the heavenly souls,
To glorify the earth with their wisdom like they did two millennia ago.

---

7. Sangam : Confluence of oceans or rivers or mind

The waves of gracious smiles from sages merged with peace into each other,

As they waited for the sages to ponder and illuminate with their knowledge.

The mighty oceans sat patiently with clasped watery hands,

As they swell and fell with each stroke of unfailing tide.

And then with the radiant sun shining behind them spreading day,

The sages smiled graciously as they began to say,

Their voice echoed from the horizon filling the anxious sky,

Time stood still the message of human glory and peace expanded to occupy the void.

The wisest sage, Confucius said,

"We are with two oceans who nurture half of humanity,

We came to the planet earth in the same century,

And gave the message of humanity and peace.

O enlightened one! O Lord Buddha,

Can you tell the world, how they can live,

With universal peace and prosperity for all?"

Buddha smiled with serene tranquility,
"God gifted humans with intelligence and the tool of reason,
It is for man to harness the might of the divine gift,
To prosper towards a life of goodness and truth."

The wisest sage, the holy master then agreed,

"O enlightened one! Your thoughts are unique,

Humans are indeed entrusted the great mission,

Of realizing with body, mind and soul – the God's vision".

Then our Island friends and the oceans which gave them birth,

Humbly joined their voices from the heart,

As they prayed and prayed again,

Beseeching the divines to give a message of human renaissance.

Again a deep silence engulfed the universe,

The cosmos seemed to be filled with energy,

The waves from both the oceans
went violently high,
And gently touched the feet of
divinity with beautiful shehnai[8]
playing with a divine song.

O planet, what a past and what a
present you possess,
And when they come together,
greeting like us two seas,

8. Shehnai : An Indian musical instrument often played in auspicious occasions

They create the future, future of peace and prosperity for all

"O wisest sage, Confucius! You have preached and preached to peasants and herders in Lu,

You preached the value of family life and that of righteousness in the heart,

And O enlightened one! Under the sprawling Bodhi tree,

You proclaimed – where there is righteousness in the heart, there is beauty in the character".

The wise sage then said,

"Yes I will sing now!

When there is beauty in the character,

There is harmony in the home"

The enlightened one, the Buddha added,

"When there is harmony in the home,
There is order in the nation,
When there is order in the nation
There is peace in the world".

In chorus, the two great sages wise and enlightened,
Blessed humanity with the song of life righteousness,
For world peace and prosperity for all.

The Islands and the oceans rejoiced in unison,

The waves and winds joined to sing the song of life in Sri Raga[9],

Om Shanti![10] Om Shanti! He-ping!6[11] He-ping!

Righteousness in the heart is the song of the planet.

□

---

9. Sri Raga : A Raga in Indian music
10. Om Shanthi : Divine peace for the world in Sanskrit
11. He-ping : World peace (Chinese)

My Song

O Mother, Mother India,
You have nursed us and grown us,
And gave us a parting mission
And an eternal message.

"O my sons and daughters,
Wherever you go,
Whatever mission you do,
Remember my children,
My three advices golden!

Always be truthful even in danger,
Sweat and sweat to acquire,
Knowledge and name,

Wherever you live enrich that land.

O, Mother we crossed the oceans and seas
With many generation of yours with your blessings,
We made new lands prosperous,
We made knowledge as the way of life
Sweat as the way of life and
We give and give to honour you

What we do is for honoring you,
We will always be children yours,
Wherever we are,
Whatever we do,
We will always be children yours!.
O Mother, Mother India.

[Composed for the participant of fifth Pravasi Bharatiya Divas Samman Awards function held on 9th Jan. 2007]

□

A Message From Mother Earth

1. Beautiful Environment leads
   To beautiful minds
   Beautiful minds generate,
   Freshness and creativity

2. Created explorers of land and sea
   Created minds that innovate
   Created great scientific minds
   Created everywhere, why?

3. Gave birth to many discoveries
   Discovered a continent and unknown lands
   Ventured into unexplored paths
   Created new highways

4. In the minds of the best,
   Worst was also born,

Generated seeds of battle and hatred

Hundreds of years of wars and blood;

5. Millions of my dear children,

Lost in the land and sea,

Tears flooded many nations,

Many engulfed in ocean of sadness.

6. Then, then came, the vision of European Union,

Took the oath,

"Never to turn human knowledge,

Against ourselves or others".

7. United in their thinking,

Actions emanated,

To make Europe prosperous and peaceful,

Born, the European Union.

8. That "Glad Tidings", captivated,

   The people of the planet of my galaxy.

   OH! European Union, let your missions,

   Spread everywhere, like the air we breathe.

[From the speech given at the European Parliament at Strasbourg on 25 April, 2007]

□

My Garden Smiles

1. My garden smiles,
   Welcoming the spring,
   Roses, beautiful roses,
   With fragrance and beauty,
   Ringing tunes of the honey bees
   Lovely scene, everywhere
   My garden smiles.

2. The enchanting scene entered into me
   blossomed happiness in my body and soul.

Variety of roses,

One lovely family of roses,

Presiding the dynamic scene,

With pleasant fragrant breeze,

My garden smiles.

3. All the roses fully blossomed towards the sky

   It was a miracle to see.

   A pleasant beautiful voice

Echoed from rose family,

O' my friend, look at the sky,

I saw the miracle of

The shining moon in formation

And the powerful venus very close

To each other belonging to the our galaxy.

4. The scene was indeed rare celeberation,

Of heavenly bodies and roses of earth,

I looked above and roses of my garden,

I looked above saw the Milkyway,

I looked around the garden,

Roses, roses and roses.

This unique festival of lights and beauty

Why, why , why, this unique scene.

This graceful event
In my garden first time,
My garden smiles.

5. Then the sweet music
Engulfed the scene all around
Emanating from garden
"It was the celebration of
flowers and heavenly bodies,

in honour of visit of poetic soul,

of our galaxy milkyway,

Yu Hsi a universal friend,

Of creative mind,"

Crossed many seas, to be with us

Welcome my friend from shining heavenly bodies,

Beautiful roses and divine music

My garden smiles.

[Composed on 28th March 2007 on the occasion of receiving the Crane Summit Supreme Honour Crown Medallion from Poet Yu His, of World Academy of Arts and Culture and Patron of World Congress of Poets]

□

Pursuit Of Happiness

I was on an unbeaten path,
All around me were joyous flowers.
My familiar world appeared strange,
In the wild were growing treasures of nature.

Blooming flowers of bounteous beauty,
Vibrant colours, dancing in abandon.
Some were buds, others older,
Some on way to sought after liberty!

Men may make merry of flowers,
Children may make playthings of them,
Dismember them or ignore to dust,
Yet all these flowers embody a truth:

Beauty of consciousness trapped in peace
Blooms of flowers show Almighty in deed.

Sowing happiness, or solemnity in need
To express ourselves everywhere we need,

To offer them to God or to the beloved,
A touch of them makes all humans go tender.
Ah, that conscious beauty of marvellous peace,
In pursuit of happiness always we need.

□

Where Is God

Bright blue sky, at RCI[12] that day
My thoughts were soaring on freedom,
Hope was their strand in radiance of peace,
Hillocks were spotted in embracing clouds,
Scientists were working, silently, heads down:

Some will be great, and others part of greater works.

12. Research Centre Imarat, Hyderabad

Finding the life around perfectly synchronized,
I asked myself: Who is the one controlling them all?
If that be God, where is He now?
Walking through that playful breeze,

I found a few squirrels valiantly gazing;
A golden bird just closed in on jasmines,
As though to talk the secrets of that hour.

I paused to ponder the blossoms of God,
Found them hinting finer new meanings.

Some were showing the signs of God,
Some others revealed part, yet others completely withheld.
Endeavours to grow, can they ever be in vain?
In a while, a robin enquired my search.
Enthused, I said: 'Indeed God!'

Swiftly taking off it said: 'You may not find here.'
Saw in its direction, myriad colours of evening clouds,
Setting sun and temple bells added meaning to the scene.

'Where is God?' an unknown voice spoke,
'Why not you look for Him, up in the orchard?'

Trees were still, and retreating light,
Birds were trying get back to nests,
Fruits were showcasing sweetness possessed,
Flowers were conveying secrets of creation.

Even glowing street lamps could not
show me an answer.

My mind was on its wings,
As if trying to search the source of
spring.
Softened and tired, I started for
home,
Suddenly a flower fell on my head,
Started to speak and said:

'O creator of dreams,
Why do you keep searching for God?
Nature is His home, purity His abode
And Life is but His blessing!
Keep loving nature and care for its
beings,
Then you can see divinity all over!'

□

God

The days were silent as if afraid of night,
Life receded like a fire without fuel
And joy and happiness just went extinct.
Was it a dance of death or annihilation?

Streets were empty, and roads were alone,
Sounds of weapons and shoes shook them all.

Men were out to kill brethren with cruelty:

Riots had broken the cage of peace and faith!

Satan was seen singing all around

As if rejoicing in His creation's misery

Ten thousand Hindus and as many Muslims

Said to have perished in tearful tragedy.

All of them were told: 'You are dying
For Khuda and Bhagwan.'
Littered bodies and liberated souls
Set out to search their saviour God.

Twenty thousand souls torn from life
In search of their Lord.
Darkness of sins spreading all over,
Yet He couldn't be traced.

The souls were engaged in travel
Eager to see a glimpse of their God.
Some of them were searching for Allah,
Rest of them were reaching for Bhagwan.

When suffering made them sulking and humble,
Suddenly there was the Light of Lord,

'Surely it is my Khuda-'

'No, no! It is our Bhagwan.'

So started a chaos all over.

Suddenly a sound thundered from Light,

'I am none of yours! All you hear!

Love was my mission and you spent it on hatred,

Killing my delight, stifling life.

'Know ye all: Khuda and Ram
Both are one, blossoming in love.'
Saying this the Lord thought for a while
Why did He make His creation so blind!

So he sent the souls back to earth
To spread the message of truth.
God is Love and Love is God
And a child was born all over again!

□

Clouds

Up in the clouds, absorbing thoughts!

All of them question me, Is this world real?

I am on the move glancing at these clouds

Sometimes in planes, otherwise in thoughts.

Scattered clouds are like clusters of buildings.

In the fairies' town of bluish sky.

Angels could be shaping these structures,

Occasionally crackling lightning to cheer the gods
Or pouring the rains to bolster our hopes!

The sun rays spread like blessings of gods
In coloured strands of flowers of heaven,

And those darkish clouds and their winding tunnels

Awaken me and make me realize myself in reality.

Yes, there is reality of power and fame too!

All these lead to familiar questions-

Where do we come from and why did we originate?

What kind of destination motivates us all?

Reminds me of my father, reciting Gibran to mother...

'Your children are not your children.

They are the sons and daughters of life's longing for itself.

They come through you but not from you...'

Ah! I wish that cloud's freedom for me!

To wander the horizons of limitless destiny,

To inhale and float in ascetic peace,

To detach from the drama of wooing for power,

To pray for love and peace of humanity.

[Composed during air travel from Delhi to Hyderabad]

□

His Best Creation

God, the Almighty decided once
That the time had come to create human life.
Millions and millions of years were spent
In designing and developing that image
With mud and clay yet with mind in its place.

At last He made a shape of that image
And worked on and on striving for perfection.

Space-time and its multi-dimensional
flow
Galloped and swallowed quite a great
reach
And He decided that the image was
ready, void of flaw,

It was time to give life to that being.
When Moon and the Sun were
together seen shining
And all the stars were pouring their
coolest rays

God commanded life to the man
And, he opened his eyes and smiled at the Lord.

Ray of that smile made Almighty happy.
Meanwhile the man said: 'O Almighty, thank you.'
God was pleased at the first actions of man
And the man in God's image arrived here to stay.
Suddenly God had a surprising feeling

That something was missing in the man He made.
In flash of a second He created a fire
And Satan emerged from the flames in no time.
Satan too bowed in reverence to God.

The Almighty said: 'O Satan, my second creation,

'Bow before man the best of my creations.'

Defiantly Satan said: 'O my creator!

I may never bow before man;

I came from fire and he came from just clay

And why should I bow before him?

'Rather he also took millions of years for a shape...'

God for the first time had a problem in hand
And pondered this issue just for a while
Then decided to integrate both of His creations
He held them together and merged them into one.

Then God commanded to Man:
'O my best creation!
I have given faculties and brain for you to deploy
Endowed with my image, use them
To defeat the Satanic temptations in you
And then come to me as one who is pure
My blessings will be there for you to win.'

□

My Mother

Sea waves, golden sand, pilgrims' faith, Rameswaram, Mosque Street, all merge into one,

My mother!

You come to me like heaven's caring arms.

I remember the days of struggle when life was challenge and toil—

Miles to walk, hours before sunrise,

To take lessons from the saintly teacher near the temple.

Again miles to the Arab teaching school,

Climb the sandy hills to Railway Station Road,
Collect, distribute newspapers to temple city citizens,
And then going to school.
Evening, collect the money before study at night.
All this pain of a young boy.
My mother you transformed into pious strength
Kneeling and bowing five times a day
For the Grace of the Almighty. My mother,

Your strong piety is your children's strength,
You always shared your best with whoever needed the most,
You always gave, and gave with faith in Him.
I still remember a day when I was ten,
Sleeping in your lap
To the envy of my elder brothers and sisters.
It was full-moon night, my world only you knew;
At midnight I awoke to tears on my cheeks
You knew the pain of your child, my mother.
Your caring hands, tenderly removing the pain,
Your love, your care, your faith gave me strength

To face the world void of fear and with His strength.

We will meet again on the great Judgement Day, my mother!

□

Whispers Of Jasmine

Breezy dawn, crackling birds,
Jasmine grove my walking track,
Fragrance in the air of this noisy alley,
Creepers dancing to tunes of cuckoos,
Gust of wind threw a strand on the path

Taken aback just for a moment
Bees are back, just about their work
Even on the fallen jasmine flowers.
Dreading that I might tread on the creeper

Gently I take a circuitous route.

Whispers from creeper touch my soul,
Halting my gait caring to listen
Toddler bud talking to mother:
Why should we blossom asks that bud,
Plucked and treated shabbily by humans.

Hearing the child, laughed, the mother

Laughed and laughed and laughed:
Look, my child, why do birds sing,
See that lawn, peacocks dancing,
Jumping deer dancing to winds,

Water birds washing their feathers
As they go gliding fashionably on water—
All these beauties adding to scene.
Joyous nature's bounteous ways
Enable humans to listen to their heart.

If deer skip jumping and peacocks miss dancing,
Beautiful water birds duck their swimming,
Soulful music neither heard nor sung,
Fragrance of flowers and cheer of their colours,

If all we avoid, humans of earth

Harder in souls, harsher in tongue,
Violence pervading walks of life,
Abrasive thinking vicious in deed,
Disturbed homes, turbulence in world.
Wanting to ward off all these hells

God willed a happier world.
To the chiming beats of musical vibrance
Shehnai and sarod, veena and tabla

All these permeate and soften the soul
Just like dancing peacocks, singing parrots,

Jumping deer, gliding ducks
Smell of roses, daisy and lily,
Lotus and jasmine caressing the soul
Making the world a place to live
To mould humans, humane in deed.

But for nature hearts harden,
Wickedness permeates even the souls,
'Tis God's will gladden thy soul.
Blossom we will, blossom we will,
Cheer up, dear bud, blossom we will!

[Composed during morning walks at Mughal Gardens, Rashtrapati Bhavan]

□

Journey To Mars

It was a full moon night at Pokhran[13],
I was at the top of sandy hill,
Soaked with moonlit night,
Radiating cool breeze in severe summer night.
Engrossed in enjoying the loving ambience,
Without the knowledge what a pleasant surprise I am for.
There was a sudden lightening,
And thunder like situations, everywhere in the desert.

13. A village in Rajasthan state

In the midst of sandy storm,
I heard a voice of calling,
It was friendly, and deep with emotions.
But the voice was not of my race.
Now we were face to face, indeed cheering face, moonlit face,
Voice like music with gesture flows from the person,
For sometime, we did not understand each other.
But my friend, with a tiny computer palm top,

My tiny computer, became medium

Now, we had a common language

1 and 0

Our communication are transliterated.

He gave the signal "I understand"

I also said, "beautiful to talk to you".

Within few minutes, Mars man and Earthman came together,

Exchanged the best of earth and best of Mars.

We talked to each other our common concerns

Astroids of Jupiter, possibility of impact on Mars and Earth.

We named each other, Mars citizen called me Earth as I called him Mars

Within few hours, we knew each other and understood the profiles of our habitat. Mars platform looks beautiful, I felt and said.

My friend offered me, a flight to MARS,

I jumped into the Mars platform, we started flying and flying.

Realised, I am, with a being, from new civilization.

Both of us at home with technologies, Mars digital display

and control in front of me, we were flying

Hypersonic regime, I showed Mars, the earth civilization.

By flying very close, Industries, IT Companies, greet him

With green fields, oceans and our heritage.

I can see Mars already, we had lot of similarities in our thinking

he wanted me to see and earth appeared as it is seen in Mars,

I saw my island Rameswaram, my native place, really he was happy to show.

Piloted from earth in Mars Platform,

He told me, I will give a surprise in Mars.

He explained after seeing many places in earth,

Mar's man said, "earth and its people are beautiful".

Mars Man, myself, decided to build a great intelligent

Prosperous and peaceful civilization by 3000 AD in Mars

We just landed Mars spaceport.

There was a great reception by Mars Citizens

What a heavenly sight;

Mars exclaimed today is Mars-Earth Day,

Let us celebrate friend.

What I saw in Mars Valley

It will be the great poetry

Of Universe, I am composing words for the poetry.

□

Blossomed To Give

O my young friends, white and pink flowers,

I witness your beauty everywhere.

Cheering the hearts and,

bringing smiles to the faces.

O my young friend, "What is your name?" I asked.

O Kalam, dear Kalam, in bluegrass they call us - Dog Wood";

But as the children of spring,

We are the April Bloomers.

"O my friend April Bloomer, What is your mission?" I asked.

We the children of spring,
Are born to give and give.
Give joy to the spirit,
Give smile to the faces,
Give happiness to the heart,
Give grace to the life.

I stretched my hand and gently touched my flower friend,
"Thank you" they whispered softly,

"Kalam you touched us with tenderness of heart,
Which made us melt in the morning dew,
We are born to give and give and give."

Then the giving flowers asked me with curious blossom,
"What does the human life give to each other?"
I was puzzled and mind ran through several fields,

I replied "O my dearest young flower,
Your life for humanity is indeed inspiring,
For a mortal being, no joy is greater than giving"

Then the young April blossom waved me goodbye,
It fell down from the mother branch,
Humbly at the feet of the great tree.
With the parting message echoing as its fragrance,
It sung "I was born to give, even as I wither away,
I will be back next spring, to give, give again."

[Composed on 17th April 2010 at Lexington, Kentucky, USA at Community Banquet organized by Bluegrass Indo-American Civic Society, Inc.(BIACS)]

□

Harmony

Cranes and seagulls were wandering the sky,
Sea waves laughing and teasing the shore.
Musing my school days my mind leapt five decades,
A small school in Rameswaram town...

Hindu or Muslim, mosque or temple,
None of those divisions nagging the thinking;

Ramanathan and I, weaving words together,
Harmonious delight of Creator's children.

Suddenly a storm arrived unannounced.
Turbaned and tweedy, known as new teacher,
Asked us to sit away awkwardly from each other.
My tears dripped; Ramanathan wept,

Nor did we get the meaning of that separation.

Sunbeams saw through the sorrowful mood,

Silently lighting our tears into gems.

Creator of all, aren't You there?

Who is this one separates us here?

Years rolled by... yet we remained friends,

Sharing the sorrows and joys of yore.

The so-called educated separated our souls,

Sowing the seeds of discord and poison.

They give not knowledge but hate and defeat;

Tell others not to heed their unwanted advice,

As the Almighty created all equal and free.

□

Unseen Hands

Far away in the Bay of Bengal,
Where sea is deep and waves are high,
Agni lands with glory and light,
Awakening the nation with acquired strength.

As the world in awe praised doyens of deed
Landed Agni, now surrounded by sea creatures
Curiously asking the source of its origin:

'Who made you Agni, and who shaped you Agni?

'Who all were behind this scintillating feat?'

Pondered Agni, gasping a while,

And delving into the past decided to speak:

'Scientists and engineers sweated it out,

'Silently merging many a day into night!

Making each part and testing my systems,

With care and delight of a creator's vision,

Hunger and sleep were submerged in mission!

'With enthusiasm and dedication in action

Melted their desires in making me alive.'

'So well the scientists made you in such fashion,'

Sea creatures quipped-in conversation!

Agni replied: 'No, not alone my friends,

Though motivation and desire are components of success,

Woven in heady mix of hard work

and technology;

Yet, wives and mothers of my creators
also

'Never allowed any problem to pierce
my makers' hopes

And prayed in silence for success
with lighted lamps

And they lighted the lamps every day
to keep up the hopes,
Hopes of millions merged with
blessings of these women.

'Beloved's love and affection of
offspring,
Blessings of elders and glow of lamps
lit by creators' wives;
I came out of the light that was quite
bright
With hope, vision and love.

'When men and women are together
Love and understanding are created
Lamp of hope and creativity blossoms
And Agni with purity and strength
emerges

'Nation grows, pride and prosperity
bloom.'

Agni looked around, took a deep breath

And announced to those who were there all around,

'I emerged from the lamps lit by the mothers and wives of my creators.'

[Composed on the successful flight of Agni IRBM Missile in 1989]

□

Our Mission Is Water

My mother called me Blue Nile
I am also named by mother White Nile
When we grew and grew we asked
Oh mother! Oh Mother!
Tell us, why did you name us Nile
Our mothers said lovingly
Oh our children!
You travel and travel
Cross mountains, forests and valleys
Thousands of miles, enriching nine countries

you reach Khartoum

You Blue and White Niles confluence with a mission,

God has commanded you to give a message

You give a beautiful message.

When we rivers confluence

Oh humanity! Why not your hearts confluence

And you blossom with happiness.

[Composed during visit to Sudan to address the National Assembly of the Republic of Sudan]